Invitation to a Mouse and other poems

ELEANOR FARJEON

Invitation to a Mouse and other poems

Chosen by Annabel Farjeon

Illustrated by Antony Maitland

Pelham Books

First published in Great Britain by
Pelham Books Ltd.,
44 Bedford Square,
London WC1B 3DU.
1981.
Second impression March 1982.

ISBN 0 7207 1322 6.

Filmset in Great Britain by BAS Printers Limited.
Printed by Hollen Street Press.
Bound by Dorstel Press Limited.

Contents

Eleanor Farjeon

Shyness often drives adults to take refuge in the friendship of much younger people, and in the beginning this was, I think, one of the strong inducements behind Eleanor Farjeon's thirst for the society and love of children. And, of course, with them her fantastic imagination could range fancy free, where with grown-ups it was obstructed by inhibitions and convention.

Whatever the reason, my aunt Eleanor's child friends were multitudinous. I well remember from the age of five the excited alarm of those crowded and noisy Christmas parties given at her mother's house in South Hampstead, organized with her brother, Harry. There was a fine feast: the table loaded with orange and green wobbling jellies, cherry-topped trifles, biscuits with white animals embossed on sweet pink, blue or brown backgrounds, there were fruit salads and sausages and crackers and lemonade that fizzed. Then came the breathless games of musical chairs and musical bumps, Harry playing the piano with marvellous energy and cunning. There were dances such as Roger de Coverley and the Lancers, Oranges and Lemons, the singing led loud and clear by Eleanor, the final tug-of-war cheered loudest for both sides by her. A candle-lit fir tree that touched the ceiling stood loaded with gifts for everyone, gifts which had been collected throughout the year.

Once a little girl in a red and black tartan kilt and plaid performed a Highland sword dance. Here I did not respond to my aunt's raptures, feeling that I could learn to hop like that and not kick the swords by mistake. But I was a shy plain child, lacking the bounce and gaiety of girls who always seemed to have partners, lovely dresses and laughing faces. Eleanor found my partners for me, kindly, quick to notice that I could not make an effort to gain friends.

In a whirl of enthusiasm she would organize yet another game—a balloon fight, the two sides sitting on the floor, and no cheating like lifting your bottom or kneeling. There were presents for losers as well as winners, given by my little American grandmother, with her soft melodious voice and her softer cheek, sitting in amiable state in her rocking chair, still full of the prettiness and charm that Eleanor so adored and could in no way emulate.

For Eleanor was podgy and without elegance. Her arms flung boldly wide, her feet came down flat. Very short-sighted, she wore small thick glasses, through which her eyes beamed, as eager to please as be pleased by the passing world: a stray cat, an old man who sold dying plants or a child's blackberry-smeared face. Her own cheeks were full, her nose bulbous, she had a soft bosom, not voluptuous but homely, very welcoming to cry on, which vast numbers of people did, both old and young, to everybody's satisfaction. Eleanor was far fuller of the milk of human kindness than anyone I have ever met.

The memorable day when she kissed our chauffeur in an excess of affability—he certainly was a very nice man, but even as a child I would never have dared—has since always sent her nephew and nieces into hoots of delighted mirth. She was a great kisser in days when this intimate form of greeting was reserved for near relatives and theatrical people.

It has never been clear to me why or when my aunt's youthful shyness wore off. Her later wide-open liveliness may have developed partly as a cover, though her mind had obviously always been so bubbling over with ideas, her interest always so quick to catch on, that it is difficult to imagine her very silent. In middle and old age she seemed a woman full of confidence: witty, sentimental, clever and somewhat jaunty. Plays, novels, songs, light operas, verses and children's tales flowed from her typewriter, sometimes successful, sometimes not, but all alive with that remarkably agile intelligence that leaped from fact to fantasy like an acrobat.

Her ability to learn and remember was extraordinary. Although she never went to school and governesses were told not to bother her, she educated herself almost entirely by reading the variety of books which her father continually bought and piled into the house. Foreign languages seemed to come effortlessly while, without any musical education except that picked up in passing from brother Harry, she could compose music for her songs and memorise whole operas and symphonies, playing them right through in her head for entertainment.

I was touched and surprised when, one day in her eighties, she said a little sadly, yet with the confidence of one who can face her own limitations, 'I have always tried to use what little talent I had to the full.' This remark had to do with the statement in the preface to *Silver-sand and Snow*, from which collection most of these poems are chosen, that—'In my youth I dreamed of being a "real" poet, but half way through my life that dream died, and whatever figments of it remained went into writing songs and verses for children.'

However, to me and probably thousands and thousands who have known her songs and verses from their early days, Eleanor is most certainly a real child's poet.

Annabel Farjeon

Invitation to a Mouse

There's pudding in the pantry,
   There's jam upon the shelf,
There's bacon in a pastry-pie
   On a dish of delf—
Mousiekin, wee Mousiekin,
   Go and help yourself!
But please, Mousie, please,
Don't touch the toasted cheese,
For if you do mayhap
Something will go snap!
And the pudding and the jam
And the pastry and the ham
Will have to stay untasted, all wasted
   on the shelf.

Mrs. Peck-Pigeon

Mrs. Peck-Pigeon
Is picking for bread,
Bob-bob-bob
Goes her little round head.
Tame as a pussy-cat
In the street,
Step-step-step
Go her little red feet.
With her little red feet
And her little round head,
Mrs. Peck-Pigeon
Goes picking for bread.

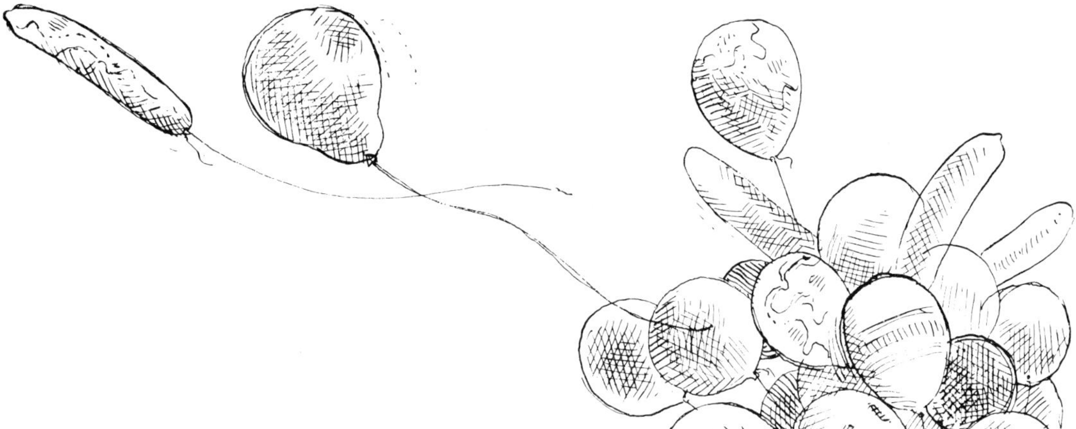

Air-Balloons

There's the man who sells balloons!
With golden suns and white full moons,
Pale green grapes and purple plums
On his shoulder, here he comes!
Just above his hat's old brim
Silver airships shine and swim.

Which to-day shall be the one?
White full moon or golden sun,
Purple plum or pale green grape,
Or will you have the other shape,
That beautiful bright oval there,
The silver ship that floats in air?

Take care not to prick it, though:
Moon and sun that bump and blow
Shrivel at the prick of pins,
And grape and plum are withered skins,
And airships crumple up like dry
Leaves, never, never more to fly.

Hey! My Pony!

What will you ride on?
I'll ride a nut-brown pony!
Hempen halter, iron bit,
Round the field I'll ride on it!
  Hey! my nut-brown pony!

What will you ride on?
I'll ride a coal-black pony!
Scarlet saddle, silken reins,
I will cross Sahara's plains.
  Hey! my coal-black pony!

What will you ride on?
I'll ride a snow-white pony!
Silver bridle, golden girth,
I will travel round the earth.
  Hey! my snow-white pony!

Sun and Wind

The old sun, the gold sun,
  With lovely May returning,
Went among the chestnut trees
  And set their candles burning.

The cold winds, the bold winds,
  Came down like Goths and Vandals,
And went among the chestnut trees
  Blowing out their candles.

K is for Kestrel

Still hangs the Kestrel there
High in the still air
When the day is fair.

So still he seems to stay
He might in the fair day
Be fixed there far away.

But presently he will
Swoop from his airy hill
And make some small bird still.

The Dewdrop

Small shining drop, no lady's ring
Holds so beautiful a thing.
At sun-up in the early air
The sweetness of the world you snare.
Within your little mirror lie
The green grass and the wingèd fly;
The lowest flower, the tallest tree
In your crystal I can see.
Why, in your tiny globe you hold
The sun himself, a midge of gold.
It makes me wonder if the world
In which so many things are curled,
The world which all men real call,
Is not the real world at all,
But just a drop of dew instead
Swinging on a spider's thread.

For the Wind

Where the Wind blows
It sows, it sows!
Seed scatters,
Grass grows,
Earth starts,
Water flows,
And Polly's Cheek is like a Rose.

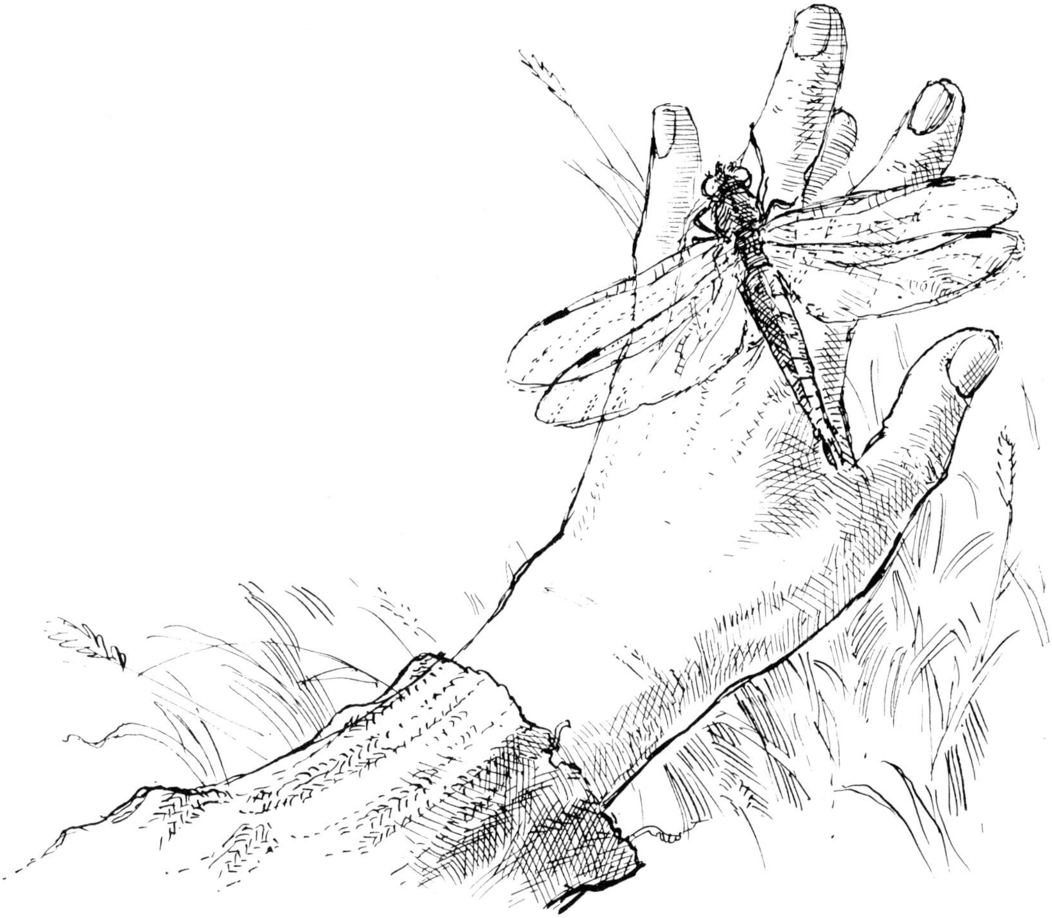

A Dragonfly

When the heat of the summer
Made drowsy the land,
A dragonfly came
And sat on my hand,
With its blue jointed body,
And wings like spun glass,
It lit on my fingers
As though they were grass.

Albatross

Hush . . . hush . . . hush . . .
The grey wind comes with a rush,
The cold wind comes with a wail,
And gliding across
The gale full sail
Lo! the Albatross.
The wind is her father,
The sea her mother,
She was born in a lather
Of foam and a smother
Of snow, long ago,
Before the ice was old.
She is careless and calm, and as cold
As a fleece of snow,
She is lovely and large, and as lone
As the Arctic Zone.
The wind
And the sea
Between them toss
Their daughter, the Albatross.

Silver-sand and Snow

Here's the soft snow again.
   See now, once more,
Drifts at the window-pane,
   Drifts by the door.

Run for your wooden spade,
   Which it may be
Silver-sand castles made,
   Drowned by the sea.

Build now your tower here;
   Let it be done
Ere it shall disappear
   Drowned by the sun.

All our best castles and
   Towers end so,
Builders in silver-sand,
   Dreamers in snow!

London Sparrow

Sparrow, you little brown gutter-mouse,
How can I tempt you into the house?
I scatter my crumbs on the window-sill
But down in the gutter you're hopping still:
I strew my cake at the open door,
But you don't seem to know what cake is for!
I drop my cherries where you can see,
I bring you water, I whistle, *'Twee!'*—
But nothing I offer, and nothing I utter
Fetches the sparrow out of the gutter.
What is it makes the road so nice
For sparrows, the little brown gutter-mice?

Mrs. Nettle and Mother Dock

Mrs. Nettle
Sits in the hedge
With her dander up
And her teeth on edge.

Old Mother Dock
Squats by the road
Ready to check
Her neighbour's goad.

Says Mrs. Nettle
All on edge,
'Nobody shan't pick
In *my* hedge!'

Old Mother Dock
Says, 'There's a fuss!
Nobody don't come
Picking *us*.'

'This is *my* hedge!'
Spits Mrs. Nettle;
'This is *my* hedge,
And I'm in fettle!

'As for them childern,
Let 'em come
Picking *my* wild
Ge-ra-ni-um!

'*My* blue harebell!
My ragged robin!
I'll pack them brats off
Throbbin' and sobbin'!'

Old Mother Dock
Grunts, 'What a stew!
You looks for trouble,
You know you do.'

Mrs. Nettle,
With bitter tongue,
Sits in the hedge
And awaits the young.

Old Mother Dock
By the roadside squats
To cure and comfort
Them cryin' brats.

The Start

The spike of daffodil,
The blue drop of a squill,

The furry silky stud
Of the grey apple-bud,

The cress of unknown seeds,
The tight brown wallflower beads,

The crocus' purse of gold,
The crumpled primrose fold,

The polyanthus star
Of red and lilac: are

The tiny treasury
Set on bush and tree

And printed on the ground
Which I this morning found.

Shall I, can I, when
At midsummer again

The fruit is set, and on
Each clump the flower new-blown

Swells the garden's store,
Love rose and apple more?

A is for Artist

The Artist sitting in the street
Chalks loaves of bread he cannot eat,
And purple hills, and emerald vales,
And salmon, and the Prince of Wales.
Give him a penny now and then;
He wants real bread like other men.

The Tide in the River

The tide in the river,
The tide in the river,
The tide in the river runs deep.
I saw a shiver
Pass over the river
As the tide turned in its sleep.

House Hunters

Birds will be house-hunting
  Soon—think of that!
Crows in the elm-tops
  And larks on the flat,

Owls in the belfry
  And wrens in the leaves,
And swifts will go house-hunting
  Under the eaves.

Moorhen will hunt for her
  House in the reeds,
Chaffinch the apple-tree
  Bough ere she breeds,
Thrush in the hollow oak,
  Sparrow won't care—
Here, there, and everywhere,
  Any old where!

Cuckoo won't trouble,
  She'll just stop and call,
But starling and nightingale,
  Blackbird and all,
Jays as they chatter,
  And doves as they croon,
Soon will be house-hunting,
  Think of it—soon!

Heigh-Ho, April!

Heigh-ho!
Let the wind blow!
Let the frost glitter, and let the rain flow!
Primula's peeping,
And scilla's done sleeping,
And daffodil's keeping the border aglow.
Buds on the lilac are starting to think,
Buds on the apple are stippled with pink,
Buds on the cherry are very near due,
Buds on the pear-tree have almost come through.
So heigh-ho!
Let the rain fall,
Let April shiver within a lace shawl!
Wallflower is breaking,
And tulip is waking
And arabis shaking her snow on the wall.
Fan of the lupin is spread like a star,
Blade of the iris stands up like a spar,
Spear of the hyacinth shatters the shield
That hardened the bosom of garden and field.

A Morning Song
(For the First Day of Spring)

Morning has broken
Like the first morning,
Blackbird has spoken
   Like the first bird.
Praise for the singing!
Praise for the morning!
Praise for them, springing
   From the first Word.

Sweet the rain's new fall
Sunlit from heaven,
Like the first dewfall
   In the first hour.
Praise for the sweetness
Of the wet garden,
Spring in completeness
   From the first shower.

Mine is the sunlight!
Mine is the morning
Born of the one light
   Eden saw play.
Praise with elation,
Praise every morning
Spring's re-creation
   Of the First Day!

Bees in Lavender

Long long pillows of lavender-flower
Either side of the narrow walk,
And the humming bees hanging hour by hour
Like small gold bells upon every stalk.

So full the lavender bushes swell
They almost meet on the narrow walk,
A mist of colour, a cloud of smell,
And gold bells humming on every stalk.

The pillowy bushes brush my dress
When I pass on the narrow walk,
And the bees take notice, no more or less,
Than I were a bee upon a stalk.

So heavy they are and so intent
On the golden hour in the narrow walk:
Lavender colour, lavender-scent,
And the bell-bees humming on every stalk.

Honey for Tea

Buzzing bee,
Buzz away, bee,
To fill the comb
For the children's tea.
Humming bee,
Bee, hum home,
To fill the cells
In the honeycomb.

All the flowers in the garden
Have emptied their bells
Into the waxen
Honey-cells,
Larkspur and lupin
And marigold,
The bag of the bee
No more can hold.

All the babes in the nursery
With sweet sticky lips
Are sucking their thumbs
And finger-tips.
Susie and Sally
And Bobby and Bill
Can eat no more,
They have had their fill.

J is for Jam

Blackberries on the brambles!
Winnie cries, 'Here I am!'
And through the thicket she scrambles
To pick the berries for jam.

And soon she has torn her pinny,
And scratched her face, poor lamb!
But what does it matter to Winnie
When she's picking berries for jam?

And soon, oh soon (need you ask it?)
The berries her small mouth cram.
She brings home an empty basket,
But she's full of blackberry jam.

Windfalls

Windfalls under the apple-trees!
Eat as many as you please.
Any apple that still lies
Shall be turned to apple-pies;
But the apple on the bough that stays
Shall be stored in the loft for winter days.

Burning the Gate

We're burning up the old blue garden gate,
The little gate as old as dead Queen Anne,
That stood between the small ground and the great,
The gardens of the master and the man.

After two centuries the blue gate stumbled
Betwixts its posts, and hung and swung askew,
The slats were worm-eaten, the paint was crumbled,
And it must be replaced by something new.

The angry hand that pushed it is forgotten,
The tender, hesitating hand about
Its latch was dust before the latch was rotten—
Now even those old touches are burned out.

Yes, now the flame is turning it to ash,
All goings and all comings by its way
Are smoking up the chimney, and a flash
Of fire wipes out two centuries in a day.

Leaves

Now when a branch hangs out its leaves
   Between the earth and sun
Through every rib and vein of green
   The light of day will run.

The leaves are not yet curtains
   Drawn when the sun's too bright,
Each leaf is still a little lamp
   That holds its fill of light.

For Mary and her Kitten

The Kitten's in the Dairy!
Where's our Mary?
She isn't in the Kitchen,
She isn't at her Stitching,
She isn't at the Weeding,
The Brewing, or the Kneading!
Mary's in the Garden, walking in a Dream,
Mary's got her Fancies, and the Kitten's got the Cream.

Dog

Whether I'm Alsatian,
Dachshund or Dalmatian,
Or any one among the Terrier crew,
However brief you've known me,
As long as you will own me
I'm Dog, that's all, my Master, Dog to you.

If you like a Setter
Or a Spaniel better,
Aberdeen or Airedale—some folk do—
Whatever breed you name me,
As long as you will claim me
I'm yours for life, my Master, Dog to you.

I'll love you, Cairn or Collie,
Beyond the point of folly,
And if I'm Mongrel, love you just as true;
Kick me or caress me,
As long as you possess me
I'm yours till death, my Master, Dog to you.

For you, I'll be so knowing!
I'll whimper at your going,
And at your coming, wag myself in two!
Trust you while I tease you,
Pester you to please you,
Your Dog, that's all, Master, Dog to you.

Outside

He's pulling on his boots!
He's going out again—
Out to the world of roots,
The whipping wind and rain,
The stinging sun that tells
On bristles and in blood,
Out to the place of smells,
And things that move, and mud;
Out where, to run a race,
Is not to hit a wall;
Out to the time of chase!
Will he whistle and call?
He's looking for his stick,
He's—Hark! his glorious shout!
I'm coming quick-quick-quick!
We're going out! We're *Out*.

Nothing

He's gone—
            and there is nothing.
Kind tones
            are nothing,
Butcher's bones
            are nothing,
The next-door cat
            is nothing,
Even his empty glove and hat
            are nothing,
The fighters in the street
            are nothing,
Friends, foes, and meat,
            all nothing, nothing, nothing—
He's gone,
            and I am nothing.

Boasting

I like biscuit,
I like bones,
I like bread and cake and scones.

I can bay
And I can bark,
I can bite and make my mark.

I can beg,
And I can bury
What I'm given deep down, very.

I can bounce
And I can bound
After balls he throws around.

I can bear,
And I can bring
Anything and everything.

I can be
A sorry beast
When my master loves me least—

When my master loves me most,
Can't I brag!
And can't I boast!

Cat!

Cat!
Scat!
Atter her, atter her,
Sleeky flatterer,
Spitfire chatterer,
Scatter her, scatter her
Off her mat!
Wuff!
Wuff!
Treat her rough!
Git her, git her,
Whiskery spitter!
Catch her, catch her,
Green-eyed scratcher!
Slathery
Slithery
Hisser,
Don't miss her!
Run till you're dithery,
Hithery
Thithery!
Pfitts! pfitts!
How she spits!
Spitch! spatch!
Can't she scratch!
Scritching the bark
Of the sycamore-tree,
She's reached her ark
And's hissing at me
Pfitts! pfitts!
Wuff! wuff!
Scat,
Cat!
That's
That!

The Old Man's Toes

Up the street,
Down the street,
My
Joan
goes—
(Mind you don't tread upon the
Old
Man's
Toes!)
She hops along the pavement
Into every Square,
But she mustn't touch the Cracks in
between
Them
There.
The Squares on the pavement
Are safe
as can
be:
One is the Sands
By the side
of the
sea;
One is a Garden where
Joan's
flowers
grow;
One is a Meadow
She
and I
know.
But the Cracks are *dangerous*,
As
Everybody
knows!
The Cracks in the Pavement are the

Old
Man's
Toes.
Any one who treads on the
Old
Man's
Corn
Will wish in a jiffy he had
Never
been
born!
For the Sea will roll up and
Suck
you
down!
And a horrid blight will turn your
Garden
brown!
And into the Meadow with an
Angry
Moo
A Big Cross Cow will come
Rushing
at
You!
Up the street and down the street
My
Joan
goes—
Here she makes a Pudding,
There she smells a Rose,
Yonder she goes stooping where the
Mushroom
grows—
(Mind, Joan! don't tread upon the
Old
Man's
Toes!)

The Lights at Night

No sooner does the sky grow dark
Than all the town breaks out in lights,
Blue and green and crimson spark
Making a thousand startling sights.

The theatres and advertisements
Dazzle the night with brilliant signs,
And high in air the world's events
Are writ in running golden lines.

The fiery pictures glow and fade,
Clusters of stars wink in and out,
The flood-lights pour their bright cascade
From domes and towers round about.

It is as though a magic spell
Had brought to life a fairy town—
Oh, what a jewelled citadel
Is London when the dark comes down!

Blind Alley

There's a turning I must pass
Often four times in a day,
Narrow, rather dark, with grass
Growing, a neglected way;

Two long walls, a tumbled shed,
Bushes shadowing each wall—
When I've wondered where it led
People say, Nowhere at all.

But if that is true, oh why
Should this turning be at all?
Some time, in the daylight, I
Will creep up along the wall;

For it somehow makes you think,
It has such a secret air,
It might lead you to the brink
Of—oh well, of anywhere!

Some time I will go. And see,
Here's the turning just in sight,
Full of shadows beckoning me!
Some time, yes. But not tonight.

On the Staircase

The stair-carpet is Turkey red,
   The banister is brown—
If only going up-stairs
   Were as quick as coming down!

It's easy before breakfast-time,
   Never thinking twice,
To slide down on the banister
   And be there in a trice.

But oh, it's hard at bedtime
   To climb the carpet-stair,
Leaving far behind you
   The world and all that's there!

Brown is the banister,
   The carpet Turkey red—
It's horrid on the staircase
   Going up to bed.

Waking at Night

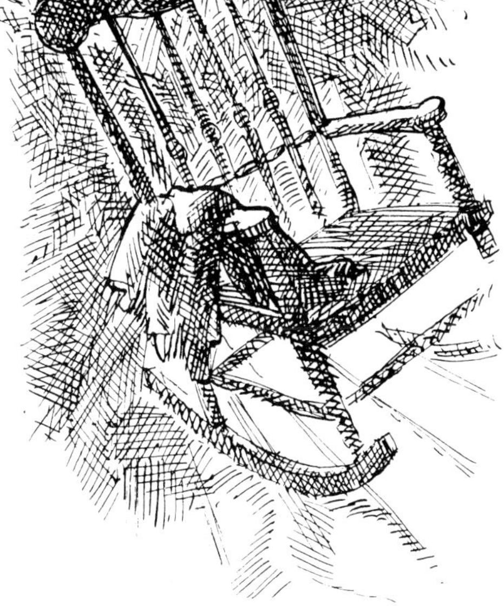

What has happened? Is this me?
Who am I? Where can I be?
Where's the fireplace? where's the door?
I can't remember any more.

If I'm me, the rocking-chair
Should be in the window there,
But the window's turned around
In the dark, and can't be found.

Strange that though the room is dark
I just know it's twisted. Hark!
That's the cuckoo-clock—how queer!—
Ticking there instead of here.

Something's happened to my bed,
Head is foot and foot is head,
And the wall has shifted quite
From my left side to my right.

Then this room is *not* the one
I know—it has come undone,
Window, fireplace, door and wall,
And I can't be me at all!

A Morning Dream

Underneath a skylight I
In my bed o' mornings lie,
Staring up through window-panes
Made dim by unremembered rains,
And always see above my face
A waving tree in dingy space.

Beyond the greeny branch up there
Flows the clear and deep blue air,
So that I almost seem to be
Drowned at the bottom of the sea
Within the cabin of a ship
Wrecked on a long-forgotten trip.

And I who lie so still abed
Might be some mariner long-dead,
While green and blue above me flow,
And living weeds wave to and fro,
And withered leaves like fishes skim
The streams of air where sparrows swim.

The Quarrel

I quarrelled with my brother,
I don't know what about,
One thing led to another
And somehow we fell out.
The start of it was slight,
The end of it was strong,
He said he was right,
I knew he was wrong!

We hated one another.
The afternoon turned black.
Then suddenly my brother
Thumped me on the back,
And said, 'Oh, *come* along!
We can't go on all night—
I was in the wrong.'
So he was in the right.

Going to Bed

Oh dear! *need* I brush my hair?
Need I get the tangles clear?
If it's tangled, *I* don't care!
Need I do my teeth? Oh dear!

Need I wash right up my arm?
Need I wash my other ear?
If it's dirty, where's the harm?
Need I wash my neck? Oh dear!

Need I untie *every* knot?
Need I fold my clothes just here?
Can't I simply on the spot
Tumble into bed? Oh dear!

Soldiers and Horses
(Early Morning)

Down the hilly avenue,
Autumn in the air,
Young soldiers riding
A double line of horses,
One horse ridden,
And one horse bare.

An eager boy beside them
Kept a level race;
Forty pair of horses
With their easy riders,
For half-a-mile of downhill
Went at walking-pace.

Half-a-mile of moving
Dark and golden flanks,
Supple pasterns curving,
Strong legs and slender
Never stopping moving
In their double ranks.

Young men upright,
Looking straight ahead,
Turning in their saddles,
Laughing to a comrade,
Masters of their horses,
The laden and the led.

House Coming Down

They're pulling down the house
   At the corner of the Square,
The floors and the ceilings
   Are out in the air,
The fireplaces so rusty,
The staircases so dusty,
And wallpaper so musty,
   Are all laid bare.

It looks like a dollshouse
   With the dolls put away,
And the furniture laid by
   Against another day;
No bed to lie in,
No pan to fry in,
Or dish to make a pie in,
   And nobody to play.

That was the parlour
   With the cream-and-yellow scrawls,
That was the bedroom
   With the roses on the walls,
There's a dark red lining
In the room they had for dining,
And a brown one, rather shining,
   Goes all up the halls.

But where is the lady
   In a pretty gown?
Where is the baby
   That used to crow and frown?
Oh, the rooms look so little,
The house looks so brittle,
And no one cares a tittle
   If it all tumbles down.

The Milk-Cart Pony

The milk-cart pony in the street
Is spotted white and brown,
He frisks his mane, he kicks his feet,
And rattles through the town.

His milk-cans glitter in the sun,
His harness clinks and rings,
The milk-cart pony on the run
Must think of lively things.

Perhaps he thinks of circus-tents
And ladies in top hats,
And orange-peel and sawdust scents,
And clowns and acrobats.

Perhaps he thinks of Derby Day
With crowds upon the course
All shouting loud *Hip hip hooray!*
Here comes the winning horse!

Perhaps he thinks of Dartymoor
Where he was once a child,
And on the purple-heather floor
The ponies still run wild.

Well, nobody knows *what* he thinks,
This little skewbald clown,
Who bears our night and morning drinks
So noisily through town!

N is for Neddy

Go, Neddy, go!
  Go up the hill,
With a bag of grist
  For the miller's mill.—
Hee-haw! perhaps I won't,
  Perhaps I will.

Go, Neddy, go!
  The mill stands still
Till you bring in grist
  For the miller's mill.—
Hee-haw! the thistles
  Are sweet on the hill.

Go, Neddy, go!
  While you eat your fill
Idle stands the miller,
  Empty stands the mill.—
Hee-haw! I'll go
  When I think I will.

White Horses

Count the white horses you meet on the way,
Count the white horses, child, day after day,
Keep a wish ready for wishing—if you
Wish on the ninth horse, your wish will come true.

I saw a white horse at the end of the lane,
I saw a white horse canter down by the shore,
I saw a white horse that was drawing a wain,
And one drinking out of a trough: that made four.

I saw a white horse gallop over the down,
I saw a white horse looking over a gate,
I saw a white horse on the way into town,
And one on the way coming back: that made eight.

But oh for the ninth one: where *he* tossed his mane,
And cantered and galloped and whinnied and swished
His silky white tail, I went looking in vain,
And the wish I had ready could never be wished.

Count the white horses you meet on the way,
Count the white horses, child, day after day,
Keep a wish ready for wishing—if you
Wish on the ninth horse, your wish will come true.

Jolly March Wind

Jolly March Wind
Blows in the street,
The street that was
So quiet and neat,
Each iron gate
Standing so still,
Curtains hung straight
At each window-sill.
    But now—
The dust is whirling!
Chimney smoke's twirling!
Gates are banging!
Curtains are hanging
    All anyhow!
Prim Miss Muffin
Is pantin' and puffin',
Her petticoat's tossed
And her hair-ribbon lost!
Old Mr. Wrangle
Is cutting a caper
After his paper
    An absolute wreck,
With his scarf in a tangle
    All round his neck!
But Jimmy and Jenny
Scream with delight,
    As hither
    And thither,
Just like a kite,
    Tumbled,
    And rumpled,
    Untidy,
    Unpinned,
They're blown home to dinner
By jolly March Wind!

Keep Still

Look, and keep very still,
Still as a tree,
And if you do you will
Presently see
The doe come down to drink
Leading her fawn
Just as they did, I think,
In the first dawn.

Hark, not a sound, my dear,
Be quiet and hark,
And very soon you'll hear
The vixen bark,
And see her cubs at play
As I believe
They played in starlight grey
On the first eve.

Look, and keep very still.
Hark, not a sound!
The pretty creatures will
Soon be around,
At play and drink, as though
They drank and played,
Cub, vixen, fawn and doe,
Ere men were made.

The Smoke

Over there
Is a little house,
Quiet as a mouse,
Or an empty hive,
Or as death.
But up in the air
From the chimney-poke
Goes the gentle smoke,
And I know that the house is alive,
I can see its breath.

Q is for Quince

The Quince tree has a silken flower,
   The Quince tree has a downy fruit,
The Quince tree is a curious bower
   Of greeny leaves and gnarly root.
Its shape is like a witch grown old,
   Its flowers like fairies, and it bears
Quinces that when their down turns gold
   Look still more beautiful than pears.
And oh, whoever smells the Quince
   Knows that the fairies must have placed
The scent there—*but don't taste it, since*
   It was the Witch who made the taste!

D is for Dairymaid

Dairymaid Doll she surely seems
To be made herself of butters and creams.
Her neck is like milk, and if you squeeze
Her hand it is soft as cottage cheese,
Her hair is yellow like when you turn
The beautiful butter out of churn,
Her cheek is brown and as smooth again
As the brown egg under the broody hen,
And when she tells you a thing, her words
Come sweet from her lips like clotted curds.

Gifts

Myrtle for the Bride,
Nettle for the Scold,
Sage for the Scholar,
And Balm for the Old.

Sweet Herbs

What shall I plant in my little herb border?
Which of these hundred sweet names shall I order?
Mallow or Marjoram, Tansy or Rue,
Lovage or Hyssop, or Call-Me-To-You?

Thyme or Sweet Cicely, which shall I take?
Shall I plant Basil for Isabel's sake?
Betony, Bergamot, Orris, Vervain,
Chicory, Woodruff, or Elecampane?

Here's Lady's Mantle, and here is Old Man;
If I cannot plant all, I must plant what I can,
But their names throw me into delicious disorder!
What shall I plant in my little herb border?

Gentle Angelica

Gentle Angelica on her green stalk
Shakes her white head in the hawthorn walk.
When her fair florets are shrivelled and shed,
Her stalk is sweeter than ever her head.

Morning Light

How beautiful! how beautiful!
The dew is on the grass,
And all the roses' cups are full,
They spill it as I pass.

The sun is very bright, and yet
The morning has no heat,
The pebbled path is silver-wet,
And oh, the air smells sweet!

It is as though I never smelt
So sweet and fresh an air,
It is as though I never felt
Such sunlight in my hair,

Or saw a diamond cobweb hang
Its curtain at my door,
Or ever heard the bird that sang
That lovely song before—

As though I saw, felt, smelt, and heard
This morning in their prime
The web, the sun, the air, the bird,
And all, for the first time!

The Garden in the Dark

The midnight that is neither light nor dark
Has stolen the garden's yellows, blues and reds;
The giant poplar now seems twice its mark
Reared up against the sky above the beds;
The stirless air
Seals shapeless groves of leaves no longer green;
Only on the young apple there
The clusters of the blossom, with a sheen
Pallid as moth-wings, float upon the eye
As though they had no contact with their tree,
And might at any moment rise and fly
Back to some distant star I cannot see.

The Meteors

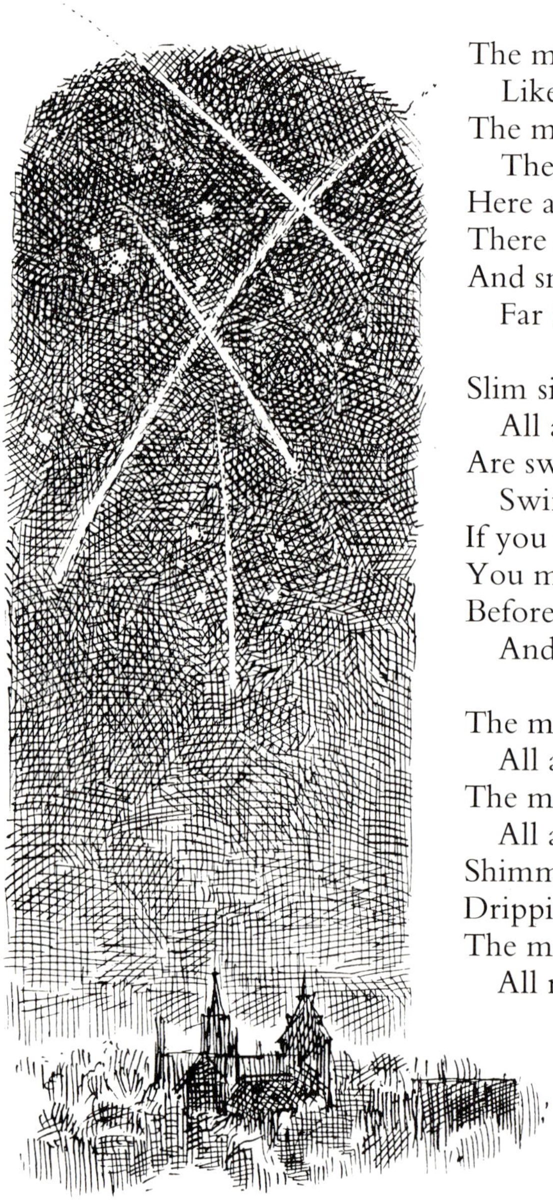

The meteors are slipping
   Like skaters on the sky!
The meteors are whipping
   Their lashes round the sky!
Here another splashes!
There another flashes!
And smashes into ashes
   Far from the sky.

Slim silver fishes,
   All and each
Are swift sly wishes
   Swimming out of reach.
If you will go fishing,
You must do your wishing
Before they finish swishing
   And fall on the beach.

The meteors are sliding
   All along the sky!
The meteors are gliding
   All about the sky!
Shimmering stems of flowers!
Dripping summer showers!
The meteors are riding
   All round the sky!

The Distance

Over the sounding sea,
Off the wandering sea
I smelt the smell of the distance
And longed for another existence.
Smell of pineapple, maize, and myrrh,
Parrot-feather and monkey-fur,
  Brown spice,
  Blue ice,
Fields of tobacco and tea and rice,

  And soundless snows,
  And snowy cotton,
  Otto of rose
Incense in an ivory palace,
Jungle rivers rich and rotten,
  Slumbering valleys,
  Smouldering mountains,
  Rank morasses
  And frozen fountains,
Black molasses and purple wine,
Coral and pearl and tar and brine,
The smell of panther and polar-bear
  And leopard-lair
  And mermaid-hair
Came from the four-cornered distance,
And I longed for another existence.

Downs

The Downs are ups as well as downs.
Down they run to the fields and towns,
But up they go to the endless sky
Where kites and clouds and pewits fly.

Quarry

When along the Downs you walk
You'll find Quarries in the chalk.
Some are caves with treasure strewn,
Some are like a white half-moon,

Some are forts and kingly halls,
Some are Moorish city walls,
And one's the cliff of the world to me,
With tides of grass instead of sea.

Ewes

The black-nosed Southdown sheep do keep
The Southdowns cropped as any lawn.
The grazing of the Sussex sheep
Begins upon the Downs at dawn;
But when the evening sky grows gold
The Ewes come down again to fold,
And sleep.

Nightingales

In Gillman's Orchard in Billingshurst
Nightingales always sing the first;
Under the apple-trees all night long
You can lie in the grass and hear their song.

And through the apple-bloom pink and white
Two or three stars will be in sight,
Like the highest, roundest, loveliest notes
Gone up to the sky from the Nightingales' throats.

Kingcups

The floods on Amberley Wildbrooks
In Spring spread out for miles,
And the Kingcups grow in the water
Like clustering golden isles.

Kingfisher

A flicker of blue
Under the sallows—
Over the shallows
A Kingfisher flew!

Ambush

The spider in its web of grey
Scarce visible in brightest day,
Now lurks in ambush, like a spy,
To catch the unsuspicious fly.

Too soon, too soon the gauzy wings
Of fragile sun-delighting things
Destroyed in Autumn's shroud will lie
Woven to catch the summer fly.

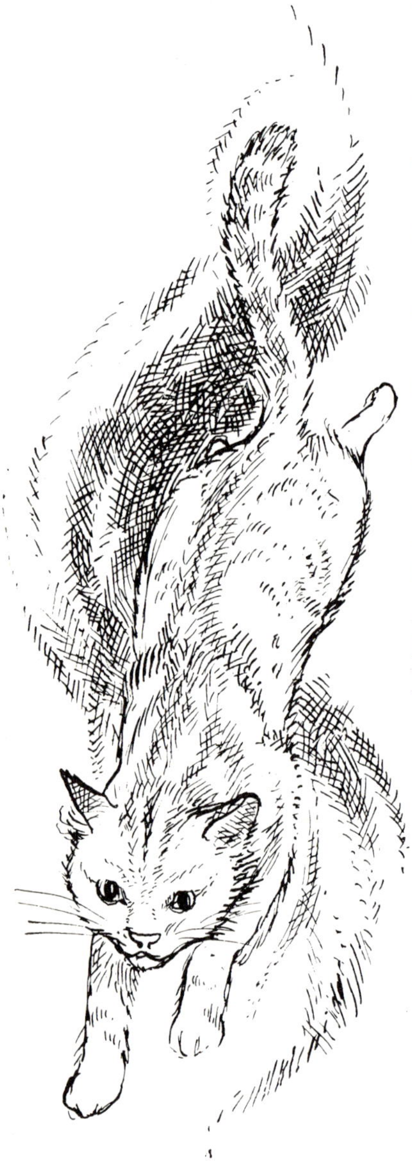

The Golden Cat

My golden cat had dappled sides;
No prince has worn so fine a cloak,
Patterned like sea-water where rides
The sun, or like the flower in oak
When the rough plank has been planed out,
Lovely as yellow mackerel skies
In moonlight, or a speckled trout.
Clear as swung honey were his eyes.

It was a wondrous daily thing
To look for, when his beautiful
Curved body gathered for a spring
That, light as any golden gull,
Flashed over the fine net of wire
Which my casement-window bars;
His leap was bright as tongues of fire,
And swift as autumn shooting-stars.

My cat was like a golden gift,
A golden myth of Grecian lore—
But things so bright, and things so swift,
Must vanish; and he is no more.

A Kitten

He's nothing much but fur
And two round eyes of blue,
He has a giant purr
And a midget mew.

He darts and pats the air,
He starts and pricks his ear,
When there is nothing there
For him to see and hear.

He runs around in rings,
But why we cannot tell;
With sideways leaps he springs
At things invisible—

Then half-way through a leap
His startled eyeballs close,
And he drops off to sleep
With one paw on his nose.

Griselda

Griselda is greedy, I'm sorry to say.
She isn't contented with four meals a day,
Like breakfast and dinner and supper and tea
(I've had to put tea after supper—you see
    Why, don't you?)
Griselda is greedy as greedy can be.

  She snoops about the larder
  For sundry small supplies,
  She breaks the little crusty bits
  Off rims of apple pies,
  She pokes the roast-potato-dish
  When Sunday dinner's done,
  And if there are two left in it
  Griselda snitches one;
  Cold chicken and cold cauliflower
  She pulls in little chunks—
And when Cook calls:
    'What *are* you doing there?'
      Griselda bunks.

Griselda is greedy. Well, that's how she feels,
She simply can't help eating in-between meals,
And always forgets what it's leading to, though
The Doctor has frequently told her: 'You know
    Why, *don't* you?'
When the stomach-ache starts and Griselda says: 'Oh.'

  She slips down to the dining-room
  When everyone's in bed,
  For cheese-rind on the supper-tray,
  And buttered crusts of bread,
  A biscuit from the biscuit-box,
  Lump sugar from the bowl,

A gherkin from the pickle-jar,
Are all Griselda's toll;
She tastes the salted almonds,
And she tries the candied fruits—
And when Dad shouts:
'Who *is* it down below?'
Griselda scoots.

Griselda is greedy. Her relatives scold,
And tell her how sorry she'll be when she's old,
She will lose her complexion, she's sure to grow fat,
She will spoil her inside—does she know what she's at?—
(Why *do* they?)
Some people *are* greedy. Leave it at that.

S is for Scarecrow

Hi, Mister Scarecrow!
  Well, bless *me*,
Ain't you a funny
  Sight to see!
Why, *I* know *you*
  Well as can be—
Your body is a broomstick,
  He, he, he!
Your gloves once belonged
  To the Parson's ma!
Your hat was the Farmer's,
  Ha, ha, ha!
Your trousers were the Cowman's,
  Your coat used to go
With Gaffer Green to market,
  Ho, ho, ho!
Hi, Mister Scarecrow!
  You may be
A scare for crows,
  But you can't scare *me*!

Bravery

The cow in the meadow
   Looks sideways at me—
   But what do I care?
   With my chin in the air,
I stare at the stile,
   Or a cloud, or a tree,
When the cow in the meadow
   Looks sideways at me.

The cow in the meadow
   Is not more than three,
   And you're not very bold
   When you aren't very old,
So I mustn't alarm her—
   She's *timid*, you see,
And that's why she always
   Looks sideways at me.

The Pear Tree

That pear tree, taller than the tiles,
Moulded in solid creamy piles
Of blossom, like a goddess stands
Dropping beauty from her hands.

Her foot is on the grassy green,
Her head against blue sky is seen,
She is not long for mortal sight
In this perfection of spring light.

But yearly, ere that form of snow
Vanishes, again I know
Beauty is herself the foam
The gods in heaven raised her from.

V is for Vegetables

The country vegetables scorn
   To lie about in shops,
They stand upright as they were born
   In neatly-patterned crops;

And when you want your dinner you
   Don't buy it from a shelf,
You find a lettuce fresh with dew
   And pull it for yourself;

You pick an apronful of peas
   And shell them on the spot,
You cut a cabbage, if you please,
   To pop into the pot.

Boredom

Oh dear! What shall I do?
Nothing lasts more than a minute or two,
Everything's silly, and nothing is fun,
And there doesn't seem anything left to be done.

Oh dear! what shall I do?
I've read all my fairy-tales seven times through,
I'm tired of my bricks and I'm sick of my train,
And my paint-box was left out all night in the rain.

Oh dear! what shall I do?
I don't *want* to go in the garden with you,
I don't *want* to sit down and play a nice game,
I want to do something that isn't the same.

Everything, everything *is* such a bore!
I don't enjoy being alive any more.
Why can't there sometimes be something that's new?
Oh dear! *what shall I* DO?

Nearly

Into the room
I crept so soft—
I scarcely breathed,
And I never coughed—
So soft, they could hardly
Know I was there,
Into the room
With oh, such care
I crept—that I *nearly*
Broke their Law,
They were just in time,
But I *nearly* Saw!

Out in the dark
I stood so still—
Like a bit of the door
Or the window-sill—
So still, they could hardly
Think of me,
Out in the dark
So noiselessly
I stood—that I *nearly*
Got the Word,
They were just in time,
But I *nearly* Heard!

Down in the wood
I tried so hard,
Hoping to get them
Off their guard,
So hard, they could scarcely
Get away,
Down in the wood
So *hard* that day
I tried—that I *nearly*
Got right through,
They were just in time,
But I *nearly* knew!

What I've Been Doing

What have I been doing, then,
To get myself in such a state?
I only stood and watched the men,
Painting Mrs. Loveday's gate,

I only went down to the brook
To catch a minnow for my jar,
I only went along to look
At Mr. Warren's motor-car,

I only climbed the walnut-tree
And slithered down along the trunk,
And reached inside the butt to see
If I could find my hat, which sunk,

I only went into the sty
To help to give the pigs their swill,
I only thought I'd like to try
To carry home a whole mole-hill,

Whatever can I have been at?
What have I been doing, then?
Nothing much—and nothing that
I shan't often do again.

Jenny White and Johnny Black

Jenny White and Johnny Black
Went out for a walk
Jenny found wild strawberries,
And John a lump of chalk.

Jenny White and Johnny Black
Clambered up the hill.
Jenny heard a willow-wren,
And John a workman's drill.

Jenny White and Johnny Black
Wandered by the dyke.
Jenny smelt the meadow-sweet,
And John a motor-bike.

Jenny White and Johnny Black
Turned into the lane.
Jenny saw the moon by day,
And Johnny saw a train.

Jenny White and Johnny Black
Walked into a storm.
Each felt for the other's hand
And found it nice and warm.

The London Owl

When in our London gardens
   The brown owl hoots at night,
Smutty walls and chimney-stacks
   All seem put to flight;

That blackness past the window-pane
   Might hold anything—
Anything wild and natural
   That moves the earth towards Spring,

Anything strange and simple,
   Any untrampled wood,
Or any broken timbered barn
   Where once warm cattle stood,

Any dark hill or reedy marsh,
   Out there when the brown owl calls—
Anything but the chimney-stacks
   And smutty London walls.

Midsummer Eve

On Midsummer Eve
They used to believe
That elves were about,
And fairies came out,
And witches on brooms,
And wraiths from their tombs,
And goblin and sprite
Made havoc all night.
And Annie, all day
So safe at her play,
Kept at home on
The Eve of St. John.
Her granny she telled her
The scent of the elder
Possessed a strange charm
To do her some harm.
It might be if she
To the old elder-tree
Went out in the dark
The fairies to mark,
The old Elder-Mother
By some means or other
Would steal her for ever,
And never, no never
No more would her granny
Set eyes upon Annie.
So as the dusk grew
More deep, and the dew
More silvery sweet,
And as the pale fleet
Of shimmery moth
Came floating like froth

Of the moon, little Ann
Followed Grandmother's plan
And stayed by the hearth.
But she thought of the path
Through sweet-scented dew-sodden
Thyme and Old Man,
Which mustn't be trodden
'Twixt seven and seven
On Midsummer Even
By wondering Ann.

The Sounds in the Evening

The sounds in the evening
Go all through the house,
The click of the clock
And the pick of the mouse,
The footsteps of people
Upon the top floor,
The skirts of my mother
That brush by my door,
The crick in the boards,
And the creak of the chairs,
The fluttering murmurs
Outside on the stairs,
The ring at the bell,
The arrival of guests,
The laugh of my father
At one of his jests,
The clashing of dishes
As dinner goes in,
The babble of voices
That distance makes thin,
The mewings of cats
That seem just by my ear,
The hooting of owls
That can never seem near,
The queer little noises
That no one explains—
Till the moon through the slats
Of my window-blind rains,
And the world of my eyes
And my ears melts like steam
As I find in my pillow
The world of my dream.

The Lost Star

Twilight came
calm and cool,
and a star
lay in a pool,
a beautiful
point of flame,
fallen so far
it had lost its name,
lost, lost
its heavenly name.

It trembled. O,
was it weeping
among the waving weeds,
and sleeping
minnows, and creeping
tadpoles? *Sso . . .*
sighed the reeds
to and fro,
sso . . . sso . . .
softly, *sso . . .*

A wind crossed
that place,
it muffled and ruffled
like grey lace
the pool's face,
the grasses tossed,
the star was shuffled
away, and lost,
for ever and ever
lost, lost.

City-Under-Water

Maureen came out of Ireland with her double-cutting
tongue.
She was crusty with the older folk, but easy with the
young.
She gave my Mother answers back my Mother thought
too free,
But Maureen gave nothing else but songs and fairy
tales to me.

She told me of a lovely lake—in her own land, she said—
With a City-Under-Water lying sunken on its bed.
Sometimes, she said, you'd surely hear the church-
bells ringing good
And clear right from the bottom to the top, indeed
you would.

She tucked me in and left me after pulling up the blind,
And City-Under-Water kept on running in my mind.
She pulled my blind because, if I was anything like *her*,
I'd find the stars were worth considering, indeed they were.

I looked out through the window where the stars
looked in again,
And the sky spread like a dark blue lake across the
window-pane.
I thought that I was looking down instead of looking up,
And the silver stars were swarming at the bottom of a cup.

I saw bright spires and shining streets and tall and
glittering towers,
And trees with silver cherries on, and silver cherry-
flowers,
And silver swallows flying where the silver fishes slid,

And silver churchbells ringing good and clear, indeed
they did.

Next day I told my Mother, and I told my Maureen too,
I'd seen City-Under-Water. Mother said it wasn't true,
I'd had a dream. But *Maureen* said, sure, did I think
because
I'd dreamed about a thing it wasn't true? Indeed
it was.

Waking Up

Oh! I have just had such a lovely dream!
And then I woke,
And all the dream went out like kettle-steam,
Or chimney-smoke.

My dream was all about—how funny, though!
I've only just
Dreamed it, and now it has begun to blow
Away like dust.

In it I went—no! in my dream I had—
No, that's not it!
I can't remember, oh, it is *too* bad,
My dream a bit.

But I saw something beautiful, I'm sure—
Then someone spoke,
And then I didn't see it any more,
Because I woke.

Snowfall

Oh, that first dazzled window-glance!
Oh, that first fall of freshest snow!
Is it a new world come by chance,
Or still the old world children know?

Where is the grass, and where's the road?
How everything is changed out there!
The bush is moulded by its load,
The tree is carved upon the air.

It is as though the house last night
Moved through the darkness, travelling
Into a magic morn of white
While nobody felt anything:

A morn all clear and crisp, that rose
Upon a land all strange and still,
A morn where ice and silence froze
The land into a trance, until

A boy with a delighted shout
The crystal of that trance should break,
And, to its promise rushing out,
Startle all the snow awake.

Sue Went to the Fair

Sue went to the Fair
With sixpence to spend—
And when she got there
It had come to an end!
The stall that sold sweets
And the tent that sold toys
Were cleared of their treats
For small girls and boys!
The big switchback stand
Was a skeleton hill,
The round-about band
Had grown silent, and still
As pictures the waggons,
The boats, and queer breeds
Of emus and dragons
And gold-saddled steeds;
The coconut sticks
Without heads stood about,
Like tall candle-wicks
Whose lights were blown out;
The shooting-booth had
Not a single bright prize
For the skilful young lad
Who could hit the bulls' eyes:
The tall spiral tower
Had fallen asleep,
And sent down no shower
Of folk in a heap;
And the motionless herds
Of red and blue swings
Hung listless as birds
That are clipped in their wings.
Oh where was the glitter

The Fair should reveal?
The grass was a litter
Of paper and peel,
The tent-ropes were slackened,
The flares were unlit,
The fairway was blackened
With cinders and grit!
And the men with brown arms,
And the girls with black hair
Who had packed up the charms
And the toys of the Fair,
Had no smiles for Sue.
She had come as their friend
But nobody knew
She had sixpence to spend.

The Brown Birds

Scant is the holly,
  The holly-berries few,
There's a bunch for the rich man
  To see his Christmas through,
And a spray or a sprig
  For the pretty-well-to-do.

But what of the brown birds
  Whom hunger maketh bold?
What of the poor birds
  A-seeking in the cold?
Oh, when the holly's scant
  And the holly-berries few,
What will the brown birds,
  The poor birds do?

Palm

As I went forth to buy holly,
  With its fruit as red as blood,
I saw a woman selling palm,
  All in its silver bud.

The sky was as blue as Easter,
  But the wind in the street did call.
She had a pinched and hungry look,
  And a child wrapped in a shawl.

'Buy my palm for a shilling,'
  She said in her beggar's whine,
'It's bitter cold for the child,' she said.
  Lord, how the palm did shine!

I paid for her living silver
  The silver that buys bread.
O Christ! Who was born with the holly,
  And rose with the palm from the dead,
Rise in the hearts of men to-night,
  For 'It's cold for the child,' she said.

H is for Hawker

At Christmas in the City
   The Hawkers with their trays
Stand close as peas inside a pod
   Along the busy ways.

They've heaps of penny presents
   To hang on Christmas-trees,
Or put into a stocking-toe
   And bulge the heel and knees.

Will you have the Jumping Rabbit?
   Will you have the Dying Pig?
Or the Little Man who lifts his hat
   And shows his fluffy wig?

Glass Snowball

Oh! oh!
My ball is full of snow.
Whirling round and round
Without a sound.
Oh! oh!
My ball is full of snow!
Fall, snow, fall
Inside my ball
On all the little people,
And the church with its steeple,
And on the pointed tree,
But you can't fall on me!

Such a scurry, such a hurry,
Such a flurry and a fuss!
We see them
But they can't see us.
There's a little tiny woman
And her dress is red,
And a little tiny man
With a hat on his head,
And a little one in blue,
And a little one in pink,
And a little one in white
Who is me, I think.

All up the hill
The little people go,
And the snow starts snowing
When *I* say so!

I wonder what they're doing,
I wonder what they're saying,
I wonder if the organ in the church
Is playing.

Will they ever reach the top?
I wonder if they will,
I wonder if they will,
I wonder why they're going
To the church on the hill.

The little one in white
Who looks like a bride,
Is she going to be confirmed
When she gets inside?
Is she going to be married
With a gold ring
While all the little people
Start to sing?
Or is it a christening
In the glistening
    Snow?
    Oh! oh!
I wish I could know,
I suppose I never will,
Why all the little people
Are going up the hill
To the church with the steeple
In the scurry of the snow,
The fuss and the flurry
    Of the snow!

A Girl Calling

Once upon a time
when the snow was falling
a girl went calling
from tree to tree:
My dove,
where can he be?
I have lost my soft-winged dove
with eyes of jet
and coral feet,
I have lost my love,
my pet,
my sweet.
Every day
he brought me a gold nut
from the filbert-tree
of the fairy king,
every day
inside the nut was shut
a present for me,
a toy, a ring,
a something, a nothing, an anything.
It kept me glad all day.
But now the ice-cold
wizard
who lives in the blizzard
has driven my dove away,
driven my dove away.
There will be no gold
nut
with a secret shut
inside its shell

till the snow has lifted its spell,
and my sweet
with the eyes of jet,
my pet
with the coral feet,
my love
with the soft white wing,
my dove
flies back in the spring.
So through the falling
snow, the girl went calling,
calling . . . calling
from tree to tree:
my love,
my love,
my dove,
where can he be?

The Children's Carol

Here we come again, again, and here we come again,
Christmas is a single pearl swinging on a chain,
Christmas is a single flower in a barren wood,
Christmas is a single sail on the salty flood,
Christmas is a single star in the empty sky,
Christmas is a single song sung for charity.
Here we come again, again, to sing to you again,
Give a single penny that we may not sing in vain.

The Song of the Fir

There was a fir
Within a wood,
Far away, far away:
It stands no longer where it stood.
Dance around the tree to-day.

It had a scent
Made sweet the air,
Far away, far away:
The sweetness is no longer there.
Breathe the sweetness as you play,
And dance around the tree to-day.

It grew between
The earth and sky,
Far away, far away:
The tree has lost its liberty
And between four walls must stay.
Breathe the sweetness as you play,
And dance around the tree to-day.

On its tip
It bore a cone,
Far away, far away:
Now that simple fruit is gone
Hang the tree with presents gay
Mid the walls where it must stay,
Shedding sweetness where you play,
And dance around the tree to-day.

Mrs. Malone

Mrs. Malone
Lived hard by a wood
All on her lonesome
As nobody should.
With her crust on a plate
And her pot on the coal
And none but herself
To converse with, poor soul.
In a shawl and a hood
She got sticks out-o'-door,
On a bit of old sacking
She slept on the floor,
And nobody, nobody
Asked how she fared
Or knew how she managed,
For nobody cared.
    Why make a pother
    About an old crone?
    What for should they bother
    With Mrs. Malone?

One Monday in winter
With snow on the ground
So thick that a footstep
Fell without sound,
She heard a faint frostbitten
Peck on the pane
And went to the window
To listen again.
There sat a cock-sparrow
Bedraggled and weak,
With half-open eyelid
And ice on his beak.
She threw up the sash
And she took the bird in,

And mumbled and fumbled it
Under her chin.
    'Ye're all of a smother,
    Ye're fair overblown!
    I've room fer another,'
    Said Mrs. Malone.

Come Tuesday while eating
Her dry morning slice
With the sparrow a-picking
('Ain't company nice!')
She heard on her doorpost
A curious scratch,
And there was a cat
With its claw on the latch.
It was hungry and thirsty
And thin as a lath,
It mewed and it mowed
On the slithery path.
She threw the door open
And warmed up some pap,
And huddled and cuddled it
In her old lap.
    'There, there, little brother,
    Ye poor skin-an'-bone,
    There's room fer another,'
    Said Mrs. Malone.

Come Wednesday while all of them
Crouched on the mat
With a crumb for the sparrow,
A sip for the cat,
There was wailing and whining
Outside in the wood,
And there sat a vixen
With six of her brood.
She was haggard and ragged

And worn to a shred,
And her half-dozen babies
Were only half-fed,
But Mrs. Malone, crying
'My! ain't they sweet!'
Happed them and lapped them
And gave them to eat.
  'You warm yerself, mother,
  Ye're cold as a stone!
  There's room fer another,'
  Said Mrs. Malone.

Come Thursday a donkey
Stepped in off the road
With sores on his withers
From bearing a load.
Come Friday when icicles
Pierced the white air
Down from the mountainside
Lumbered a bear.
For each she had something,
If little, to give—
'Lord knows, the poor critters
Must all of 'em live.'
She gave them her sacking,
Her hood and her shawl,
Her loaf and her teapot—
She gave them her all.
  'What with one thing and t'other
  Me fambily's grown,
  And there's room fer another,'
  Said Mrs. Malone.

Come Saturday evening
When time was to sup
Mrs. Malone
Had forgot to sit up.

The cat said *meeow*,
And the sparrow said *peep*,
The vixen, *she's sleeping*,
The bear, *let her sleep*.
On the back of the donkey
They bore her away,
Through trees and up mountains
Beyond night and day,
Till come Sunday morning
They brought her in state
Through the last cloudbank
As far as the Gate.
  'Who is it,' asked Peter,
  You have with you there?'
  And donkey and sparrow,
  Cat, vixen and bear

Exclaimed, 'Do you tell us
Up here she's unknown?
It's our mother, God bless us!
It's Mrs. Malone
Whose havings were few
And whose holding was small
And whose heart was so big
It had room for us all.'
Then Mrs. Malone
Of a sudden awoke,
She rubbed her two eyeballs
And anxiously spoke:
'Where am I, to goodness,
And what do I see?
My dears, let's turn back,
This ain't no place fer me!'
  But Peter said, 'Mother
  Go in to the Throne.
  There's room for another
  One, Mrs. Malone.'

The Sands

The sands are running out, old Time,
The sands are running thin,
Oh, turn the glass about, about,
And let the young time in.

The sands are soon to pass, old Time,
The sands are running through,
Oh, turn the glass, oh, turn the glass,
And let old sands run new.

Index